The Little Brainwaves investigate...

ANIMALS

Illustrated by
Lisa Swerling and Ralph Lazar

DK

LONDON, NEW YORK,
MELBOURNE, MUNICH, and DELHI

Written and edited by Caroline Bingham
Designed by Jess Bentall

Illustration Lisa Swerling & Ralph Lazar
Picture researcher Rob Nunn
Production editor Siu Chan
US editor Margaret Parrish
Creative director Jane Bull
Category publisher Mary Ling
Consultant Kim Bryan

First published in the United States in 2010 by
DK Publishing, 375 Hudson Street, New York, New York 10014

Little Brainwaves Artwork and Lazar Font
Copyright © 2010 Lisa Swerling and Ralph Lazar

Text, layouts, and design
Copyright © 2010 Dorling Kindersley Limited
10 11 12 13 14 10 9 8 7 6 5 4 3 2 1
177756—04/10

A catalog record for this book
is available from the Library of Congress
ISBN 978-0-7566-6280-6
Color reproduction by MDP, UK
Printed and bound by Toppan, China

Discover more at
www.dk.com

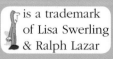

is a trademark
of Lisa Swerling
& Ralph Lazar

The Little Brainwaves investigate...

ANIMALS

Illustrated by
Lisa Swerling and Ralph Lazar

Contents

Spot the Little Brainwaves!

The Little Brainwaves are little people with big ideas. With their help, this fascinating book takes an extremely informative look at the amazing world of animals. Each of the colorful characters below appear on every page of the book. Have fun spotting them!

Ed the explorer

Vince the vet

Mop & Bop, the zookeeper twins

Goobie

Naughty Ned

Mr. Strong

Hidden Harry

Brianwave

What is an animal?

All living things fall into two main groups. They are either an animal or a plant. They all grow, feed, and have young. But animals can do something plants can't do—they can move (or at least most of them can)! Join the Little Brainwaves to find out more.

WHAT KIND OF ANIMAL?
Animals can be split into two groups: the largest group are the invertebrates (or creepy crawlies), while vertebrates (animals with backbones) can be divided into mammals, birds, fish, reptiles, and amphibians.

Vertebrates

MAMMALS
We are mammals. So are lions and tigers and mice and whales and seals. Mammal mothers feed their young with milk.

BIRDS
Birds can be found everywhere and their songs are often heard at dawn. Birds have feathers and most can fly.

REPTILES
Most reptiles lay eggs. They have dry skin that is covered with protective scales or horny plates. Snakes are reptiles.

AMPHIBIANS
Amphibians have soft skin and must keep it moist. Most amphibians breathe air as adults, but begin their lives in water.

FISH
Fish spend their lives in water. They have fins and a protective covering of scales. Most breathe using gills.

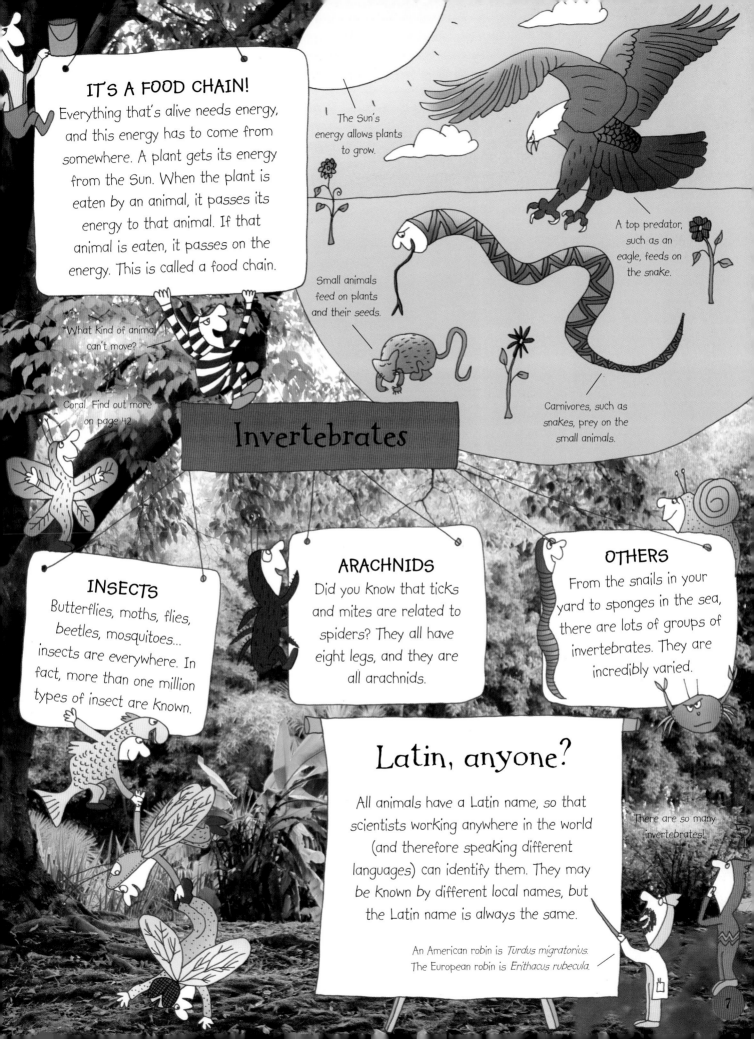

IT'S A FOOD CHAIN!

Everything that's alive needs energy, and this energy has to come from somewhere. A plant gets its energy from the Sun. When the plant is eaten by an animal, it passes its energy to that animal. If that animal is eaten, it passes on the energy. This is called a food chain.

The Sun's energy allows plants to grow.

A top predator, such as an eagle, feeds on the snake.

Small animals feed on plants and their seeds.

Carnivores, such as snakes, prey on the small animals.

*What kind of animal can't move?

Coral. Find out more on page 42.

Invertebrates

INSECTS

Butterflies, moths, flies, beetles, mosquitoes... insects are everywhere. In fact, more than one million types of insect are known.

ARACHNIDS

Did you know that ticks and mites are related to spiders? They all have eight legs, and they are all arachnids.

OTHERS

From the snails in your yard to sponges in the sea, there are lots of groups of invertebrates. They are incredibly varied.

Latin, anyone?

All animals have a Latin name, so that scientists working anywhere in the world (and therefore speaking different languages) can identify them. They may be known by different local names, but the Latin name is always the same.

An American robin is *Turdus migratorius*. The European robin is *Erithacus rubecula*.

There are so many invertebrates!

What are mammals?

There are around 5,000 species of mammal, from tiny shrews and bats to huge, water-based mammals such as the blue whale. Certain features set mammals apart from other animals.

Whales and dolphins don't have fur, although some have bristles around their mouths.

What mammals don't have fur?

THEY HAVE LIVE BABIES
Most mammals give birth to live babies. Many of these babies look like their parents and are fully developed, but they are miniature versions and require a lot of care before they are ready to survive on their own.

The blue whale is a marine mammal. Learn more about marine mammals on page 22-23.

(BUT SOME LAY EGGS!)
There are five egg-laying mammals: four species of echidnas, and the duck-billed platypus. (The echidna is also known as the spiny anteater.) These mammals lay eggs with soft, leathery shells.

A BONY INSIDE

Mammals have a bony skeleton with a backbone, like all vertebrates. However, mammal skeletons have a jaw hinged to the skull and a lower jaw that is one bone. These things make the jaw good for cutting or slicing and chewing food.

A FUR COAT

Most, although not all, mammals have fur. It provides a protective, warm coat. Fur can also help an animal to hide—from prey or from a predator.

STAYING WARM

Mammals are warm-blooded. That means that they make their own body heat, using the food they have eaten as fuel.

IT'S TIME FOR YOUR MILK!

Mammals suckle their young, the mother producing milk to nourish the baby. Most mammal babies suckle the milk through teats on the mother's chest.

9

Mothers and babies

Mammals (or at least most of them) give birth to live babies. Humans are mammals, and lots of other mammal mothers take care of their babies as we do—feeding them, keeping them warm, and teaching them how look after themselves in the world.

TIME FOR NURSING

A mother rabbit may have up to nine babies at a time. They are born blind and without fur, but use their sense of smell to find food—milk from their mother. The mother usually has enough teats to allow all her young to feed at once.

DANGEROUS GRUB

Like other mammals, baby meerkats feed on milk. As they get older, they move onto insects. These can be poisonous and dangerous to eat, so a pup's mother (and other meerkats in the group) show it how to catch and kill and feed safely.

Baby rabbits are called kits.

MARINE MAMMAL MOMMY

Dolphins are mammals that live in water. A dolphin breathes air through nostrils on top of its head, and females give birth in water. As soon as her baby is born, she helps it to the surface to breathe.

Rabbits nibble all kinds of plants.

They like carrots because carrots taste sweet.

IT'S A BABY KOALA

A koala baby, a joey, is smaller than your little finger at birth. And, like rabbit kits, it is bald and blind. But it can still drag itself into its mother's pouch where it drinks milk, keeps warm, and grows.

Is it an ape or a monkey?

Monkeys and apes belong to a large group of mammals called primates. Primates are good climbers, and some spend their whole lives in trees. They have strong arms and legs and long, grasping fingers. Many are playful and intelligent. But how do you tell an ape from a monkey?

Chimpanzees have a large brain and are among the most intelligent of all animals.

APES USE TOOLS

Few animals use tools, but chimpanzees will regularly pick up a stick, strip off its bark, and use it to poke a termite nest. They can then pick off the termites to eat. They will also use stones to crack open nuts. Other apes have been seen to use tools—but only two species of monkey have.

Gorillas are the largest apes.

WHAT MAKES AN APE?

There are 21 species of ape. Chimpanzees are apes. So are gibbons. And human beings.
* Most are larger than monkeys.
* They have no tail.
* The forelimbs are longer than the hindlimbs (except humans).
* Chests are rounded.

ONLY MONKEYS HAVE TAILS

Most monkeys have long tails, and some have tails they can use to grasp as they move through the trees. It's a little like having an extra arm and very useful—it is known as a "prehensile" tail. Not all monkeys have a prehensile tail. This one doesn't.

TIME FOR GROOMING

One thing that apes and monkeys all love to do is to groom. Regular grooming helps to keep a primate's coat clean and helps the animals to bond.

Mona monkeys belong to a group known as "old world monkeys."

WHAT MAKES A MONKEY?

There are about 248 species of monkey. Monkeys include baboons and macaques.
* Most have tails.
* All four limbs are a similar length.
* They rarely walk on two limbs.
* Monkeys have flat chests.

MONKEYS WALK ON ALL FOURS

Most monkeys will use all four limbs for walking, while apes can more easily walk on two. Monkeys are so well adapted to walking in this way that they can easily run along branches that are high above the ground.

13

Look closer: orangutan

The orangutan is one of the great apes and is the largest tree-dwelling mammal in the world. It is perfectly adapted to tree life, with arms that have a long reach and grasping feet. These are the only apes that live in Asia.

Orangutans have eyes set at the front of their faces, just like we do. They have good vision and see in color.

HOW OLD DO THEY GET?

Wild orangutans can live to the ripe old age of 45. Most of the time they live alone, but young orangutans are dependent on their mothers until they are about five.

I CAN DO THAT, TOO

Orangutans are intelligent. In captivity, they will copy the actions of their keepers. In the wild, they build nightly nests from leaves and sticks and will also use sticks as tools.

IT'S A BOY!

A male orangutan looks very different from a female. He grows a moustache and beard and has much larger cheek pads as well as a big throat pouch.

FINGERS AND THUMBS
Like other primates, including humans, orangutans have opposable thumbs. This means they can touch their little finger with their thumb. Unlike us, orangutans have opposable toes on their feet as well, with their big toe acting like a thumb. It helps them to grip and grab when in the trees.

The orangutan has incredibly flexible joints that allow it to turn, bend, and reach farther than any other primate. It is a master climber!

All orangutans have red hair.

An orangutan's arms are much stronger than its legs.

I'M HUNGRY!
Orangutans love to eat fruit, peeling off the skin just like we do, but they will also tuck into leaves and flowers, insects, and even an egg (if they find a nest).

I CAN REACH IT!
Orangutans have amazingly long arms. Males can have an arm span of more than 6½ ft (2 m), which is longer than they are tall. That's a useful stretch when they are reaching for particularly tasty fruits.

LIVING IN THE TREETOPS
The word orangutan means "person of the forest" in Malay. This is a fitting name, since wild orangutans spend nearly all their lives in the treetops. Only the males tend to venture down to the forest floor. The females even give birth in the treetops!

Big cat, little cat

Cats are efficient hunters. Big or small, they have sharp canine teeth, whiskers that are incredibly sensitive to touch, keen night sight, and fur that provides good camouflage when they stalk their prey.

GOING HUNTING

A wild cat will prey on what it can catch. Depending on the cat's size, this may be anything from rodents and birds to deer, wild pigs, and cattle. A pet cat hunts instinctively, catching mice, birds, and frogs. Both wild cats and pet cats hunt by crouching and movng slowly.

All cats will take the time to stretch their bodies after a nap. It helps to wake up their muscles.

The largest wild cat is the tiger. An adult tiger can eat up to 90 lb (40 kg) at one meal.

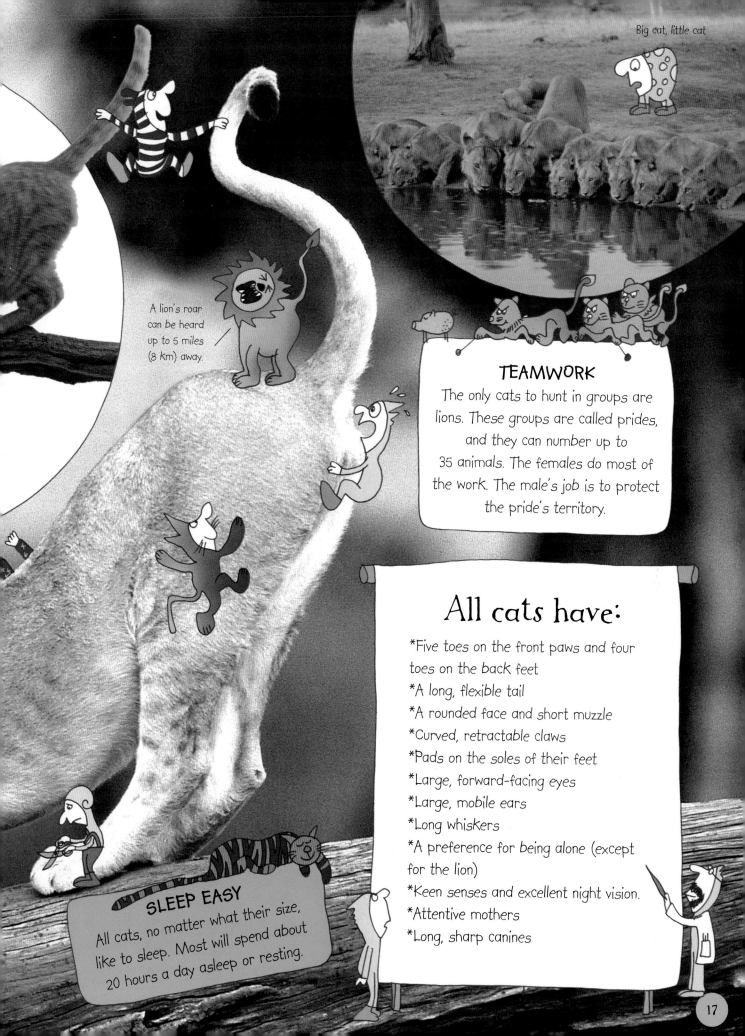

A lion's roar can be heard up to 5 miles (8 km) away.

TEAMWORK

The only cats to hunt in groups are lions. These groups are called prides, and they can number up to 35 animals. The females do most of the work. The male's job is to protect the pride's territory.

All cats have:

*Five toes on the front paws and four toes on the back feet

*A long, flexible tail

*A rounded face and short muzzle

*Curved, retractable claws

*Pads on the soles of their feet

*Large, forward-facing eyes

*Large, mobile ears

*Long whiskers

*A preference for being alone (except for the lion)

*Keen senses and excellent night vision.

*Attentive mothers

*Long, sharp canines

SLEEP EASY

All cats, no matter what their size, like to sleep. Most will spend about 20 hours a day asleep or resting.

Look closer: family life

You learn from your parents, and so do many other animals. Parents across the animal kingdom protect, teach, and feed their babies. Female elephants make particularly attentive parents.

Newborn elephants may drink more than 3 gallons (11 liters) of milk a day.

FAMILY GROUPS
Elephant herds contain related females and their young, with the largest female (known as the "matriarch") in charge. Males leave the herd once they are old enough to look after themselves.

A calf will suckle its mother until it is four or five years old.

LIFE'S LESSONS
All the skills a baby elephant needs to survive in the wild are learned from its mother, aunts, and older siblings. This tight family group all help to look after the youngest elephants, which allows the mothers the time to find the food they need.

Elephants are herbivores: they eat plant matter.

EARLY YEARS
Elephants have one calf, which is usually born at night. The first couple of years of a calf's life are the most dangerous, and it needs its mom to help it find its way around and teach it to find food and water.

An elephant can reach the age of 70

Males leave the herd between the ages of 12 and 15

When one of the herd dies, the other elephants show signs of sadness and loss.

HUGGED BY A NOSE
An elephant communicates with her calf, and her herd, using sound and with constant body contact, and the trunk plays a big part in this. On meeting, elephants use their trunks to smell each other. Quite often, one will place its trunk tip in the other's mouth.

I'LL USE MY TRUNK!
The trunk is used to suck, gather food, throw dust over the elephant's back, dig, to reassure other elephants, to smell, and as a hand... in fact, its uses are almost infinite.

A trunk has more than 40,000 muscles.

Now I see you!

Many mammals are masters of disguise. Whether they are hunters, needing to creep up on prey, or the hunted, needing to hide, their appearance helps them to disappear, and it can make a difference between life or death.

A seal pup's fluffy white coat helps to hide it from the polar bears that would like to eat it.

Why doesn't it just swim away?

Pups don't float well and they have to learn to swim.

HIDE AND SEEK
A polar bear crouches by an air hole in the ice, pale against the white snow. A newborn deer lies in dry grass, its brown coat helping to hide it. The way an animal can disappear into its background is seen throughout the animal world. It is called camouflage.

It's summer!

I'D LIKE A CHANGE

Some animals will change color with the seasons. The Arctic fox has a white coat in the fall and winter, while in the spring and over the summer it turns brownish gray. The colors help the fox hunt its prey more easily.

It's winter!

They look very different – it's bigger in winter. Is it the same fox?

An Arctic fox's winter coat is thicker than its summer coat.

TRICKS WITH PATTERNS

Why is a zebra striped? Lions, who hunt zebra, are color blind, so a mass of striped zebra blends into the background, giving more protection to the zebras that stay close to the herd.

Mammals at sea

Our planet's largest mammals (whales!) don't walk on land; they swim in the sea. Many whales are huge. An adult blue whale is the size of a large truck, while a humpback's flipper is the length of a family car.

Sperm whales have the largerst brain of any animal.

A dolphin is a toothed whale.

DOES IT HAVE TEETH?
Whales can be split into two groups: those that have teeth and those that don't. Toothed whales like this sperm whale have teeth that are all the same shape.

Baleen plates

Barnacles

Barnacles attach themselves to the skin of some whales. This doesn't harm the whale.

Barnacles are small shellfish.

HOW DO TOOTHLESS WHALES EAT?

Whales without teeth are called "baleen" whales. They sift tiny shrimplike creatures from the sea through baleen plates. These are rows of stiff hairs that grow down from their top jaw. The northern right whale, shown here, is a baleen whale.

THE WOLF OF THE SEA

The orca, or killer whale, is an efficient hunter. This toothed whale hunts fish, squid, penguins, and sea lions, as well as young blue whales.

Other sea mammals

More mammals than you might think live in (or depend on) the sea. They include:

* Bottlenose dolphins are perhaps the best-known of all 36 different types of marine dolphin.

* Sea otters spend most of their time in water—they even sleep on their backs at sea.

* Dugongs are also known as "sea cows" because they graze on sea grass.

* Walruses are protected from the icy waters of the Arctic ocean by a thick layer of blubber.

Inside a beaver's lodge

Beavers are rodents—they are related to rats and mice, but they are far larger. Like rats and mice, they have teeth made for gnawing. However, their teeth can gnaw through thick tree trunks, providing them with the branches they need to build a home.

A BEAVER'S HOME

Beavers build dens on riverbanks, or they may build a lodge in a lake. For this, they drag sticks to their chosen site and build up a large mound. They then chew an underwater entry and create a dry chamber. An outer coating of mud freezes in the winter, providing a hard, protective surface.

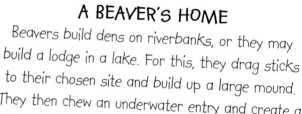

I'VE FELLED ANOTHER TREE!

Beavers have incredibly strong front teeth that never stop growing and are perfect for cutting through wood. In fact, they need to keep gnawing to stop their teeth from getting too long. And gnaw they do. One beaver can take down 200 trees a year!

There will usually be two dens, one for drying off, one a dry area.

CHANGES TO THE LANDSCAPE

A beaver family may dam a river to create a pond for a lodge. Two beavers can build a basic dam in a few days, but will then build it up. Some dams reach amazing sizes—a large one can be the height of two cars piled on top of each other.

The dam makes a wetland, changing the area it's in and attracting birds and animals that wouldn't otherwise be there.

A PLACE OF SAFETY

A lodge provides a safe home because it is impossible for predators to enter as the entrance and exit are underwater. Once inside, the North American beaver is safe from the bears, wolves, and coyotes that might choose it as prey.

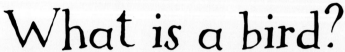

What is a bird?

Birds are the only animals that have feathers. They also have bills (but they don't have teeth!). There are about 10,000 different species of bird around the world, in an amazing array of colors. Most can fly.

Family groups

Birds are divided into groups of similar kinds. Here are some of them:

* Water birds, such as pelicans and their relatives, are strong swimmers. Some eat plants, and some eat fish.

* Flightless birds include penguins. Although they can't fly, penguins can speed though water chasing their next meal.

* Birds of prey include eagles and vultures. These hunt during the day, killing, or feeding on animals that are already dead.

* Owls are birds of prey, too, but they usually hunt at night. They swoop down silently on their prey, catching it in their sharp talons.

* Passerines, or perching birds, such as this robin are known for their songs. Most bird species are passerines.

This peregrine falcon is one of the fastest birds in the world.

When it dives on prey, a peregrine can travel at more than 100 mph (160 kph).

BILL TALK
Birds have bills, instead of jaws with teeth. These are different shapes, depending on what they are used for. Seed eaters have short, cone-shaped bills, while birds of prey have sharp, hooked bills.

FEATHERY FACTS

Believe it or not, feathers are made from the same material as your hair: keratin. (It is also found in a reptile's scales.) Birds constantly clean and oil their feathers to keep them in good shape. This is known as preening.

Penguins are one of the few birds that cannot fly.

This is what a feather looks like under a microscope.

A bird's feathers help to shape its wing so air flows around it and gives the bird lift.

Many birds have feathers that weigh more than their skeletons!

A STARLING'S SKELETON

Many scientists now believe that birds are related to dinosaurs.

A bird's wide breastbone acts as an anchor for the flight muscles.

HOLLOW BONES

A bird's bones are full of holes! This makes them light in weight—if the bones were solid, the bird wouldn't be able to fly.

Birds' eggs

All birds lay eggs. Depending on the species, these can be as small as a pea or as large as a melon. A chick grows inside a fertilized egg. When it's big enough, it pecks its way out. Cheep!

WHAT'S IN A SHAPE?

Some birds lay eggs that are almost round. Others lay long eggs. Many seabirds lay eggs that are pointed. This is helpful because some seabirds lay eggs on cliff faces. The shape means that if the egg rolls, it rolls around in a circle and doesn't crash into the sea below.

LITTLE AND LARGE

The smallest egg is laid by the world's smallest bird, the bee hummingbird. This tiny creature is little bigger than a bee and buzzes like one when it flaps its wings. Its egg is pea-sized. The largest egg belongs to the ostrich. You could fit more than 4,000 bee hummingbird eggs into one ostrich egg.

It's a bee hummingbird's egg.

It's tiny!

COLOR WAYS

Birds lay their eggs out in the open, or in holes, or in nests. Eggs laid in the open tend to be speckled so they blend in with the surroundings. But eggs laid in holes tend to be bright white or blue so the parent birds can find them.

Seabirds' eggs come in lots of different patterns so parents can recognize their own eggs among the thousands on the cliff.

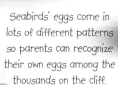

HERE I COME!

Chickens grow inside their shells for 21 days before pecking their way out. Hatching is an exhausting process for a chick, since it has to peck at the shell hundreds of times to make a hole. Just before they are ready to come out, chicks will often begin to cheep to their mother from inside the egg.

LET'S TAKE A LOOK INSIDE AND WATCH A CHICK GROW.

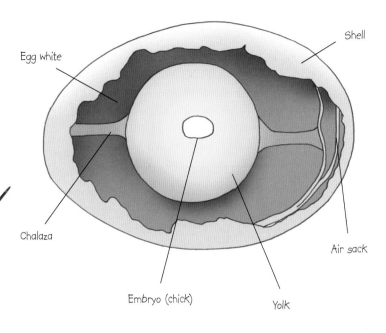

Egg white

Shell

Chalaza

Air sack

Embryo (chick)

Yolk

Eggs are laid big end first.

A chicken can lay an egg a day.

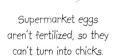
Supermarket eggs aren't fertilized, so they can't turn into chicks.

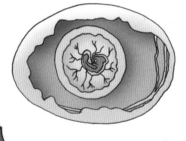

DAY 4 The embryo develops quickly and there are already buds for the legs and wings. The yolk provides the chick's food.

DAY 10 The head develops at the larger end of the egg. The chick now looks like a bird, with a beak. It still uses the yolk for food.

DAY 20 By now, the chick has little room and is in position to break out of the egg, using a special egg tooth. Hatching occurs on day 21.

Birds' nests

From hollows made in the sand to simple cup-shaped dwellings to shared nests that engulf telephone poles, there are an amazing variety of birds' nests. Take a look at some of them with the Little Brainwaves.

WHY BUILD A NEST?

Birds lay eggs, and they need a safe place to lay those eggs and a warm place in which the eggs can develop. A nest is perfect for this. However, not all nests provide this protection— some birds simply scrape a shallow dip in the ground.

WHAT SHALL I USE?

Nests may be built from materials that range from stones to mud to twigs to found items such as string. Some birds, such as swallows, use saliva to glue their mud nests together. Feathers and lichen are then often used to line a nest for warmth and softness.

The masked weaver bird builds its nest from green grasses.

This songbird has built a cup-shaped nest in the fork of a tree branch.

Long-tailed tits use cobwebs to hold their moss nests together.

Some birds lay eggs directly on the ground, using no nest.

Types of nest

This model of an ovenbird's mud nest has an open top to show the nest's interior.

Woodpeckers drill holes into tree trunks, hollowing out a space for a nest.

This Steller's sea eagle has built an immense platform nest at the top of a tree. The nest is called an aerie.

African sociable weavers build massive communal nests. Up to 100 familes may share a nest.

I CAN'T BE BOTHERED

Owls are not good nest builders. Instead, depending on the species, they will choose a hole in a tree trunk or a cavity in a log. Some nest close to, or at, ground level. Others move into abandoned burrows.

What is a reptile?

If asked to name a reptile, most people will mention a crocodile or a snake. There are actually around 9,000 species (types) of reptile. All have features in common. Can you name the most noticeable? It's their scaly bodies!

WE HAVE SCALY SKIN

Reptiles are covered with a protective layer of scaly skin. The scales actually contain the same substance as is in your fingernails, which gives them strength. (It's called keratin.) Learn more about how this skin is regularly replaced on pages 34-35.

Cameleons belong to the lizard group of reptiles.

A reptile's scales are waterproof.

Family groups

Reptiles can be divided into four main groups:

* Snakes and lizards
* Crocodiles
* Tortoises and turtles
* Tuataras

Baby ball python

Paraguayan (common) caiman

These turtles are warming themselves in the Sun's rays.

A chameleon's tail can be used to grasp branches.

BASKING IN THE SUN

Reptiles cannot make their own heat—they are cold-blooded. That doesn't mean that their blood is cold. It means their body temperature depends on their surroundings. So sometimes reptiles will lie in sunlight to warm up, moving into shade if it becomes too hot.

THEY LAY EGGS!

Many reptiles are egg layers (some reptiles give birth to live young). Most reptile eggs have a tough, leathery shell, and they will be laid in burrows or in dead plant matter. Reptile young are usually left to look after themselves from birth.

A new skin

We lose millions of dead skin cells each day, but since we don't have to shed skin in large pieces, we don't see it happening. Reptiles are different. Their scales don't grow, so a reptile has to shed its skin in order to grow.

IS IT GOING TO SHED?
Shortly before a snake is ready to lose (or slough off) its skin, it will change color, often becoming duller, while its eyes will appear cloudy. Snakes usually don't eat around this time. To break the skin, it will rub its head against a rock or tree trunk.

The scales that appear beneath the shed layer are larger.

Is it possible to tell from a shed skin what snake it came from?

Yes, sometimes! A snake's body patterns may leave clues or markings on the shed piece.

A new skin

ALL IN ONE

Many snakes shed their skin in one piece, with the growth in their bodies forcing the outer dead skin to split. Other reptiles—such as lizards and turtles—leave behind bits and pieces as they shed.

A snake cannot see well just before it sheds, and this makes it vulnerable to predators.

The eye is covered by a clear scale, called a spectacle.

Immediately after shedding its skin, a snake's coloring will appear brighter.

CAN THEY LIVE WITHOUT SKIN?

Reptiles don't actually shed all their skin, just the dead outer layer. A healthy snake may shed six times a year, but it varies depending on age and diet and species.

What is an amphibian?

Like reptiles, amphibians are cold-blooded, but their skin has no scales and is usually soft and moist (some toads have skin that is as tough as leather!). Most amphibians live in damp surroundings, which helps to keep it this way.

Around 380 species of salamander have no lungs at all!

How do they breathe?

Some through their skin and mouths. Others have external gills.

FROM WATER TO LAND TO WATER

Most amphibians spend part of their lives in water and part on land. The majority begin life as larvae in water and move onto land as adults. However, they always remain near water, since they dry out quickly if they do not stay damp.

Family groups

There are three main groups of amphibian: frogs and toads, newts and salamanders, and wormlike caecilians.

Great plains toad

Ringed caecilian

Red-spotted newt

Caecilians are rarely seen because they live in soil burrows or under water.

TAKE A BREATH

Although they have lungs, some amphibians (such as this frog) are also able to breathe through their skin (that's very useful for a frog when it dives under water). Some can even take in oxygen through the roofs of their mouths.

FIRE SALAMANDER

What is an amphibian?

DO THEY GET EATEN?

If their skin is so soft, how do amphibians protect themselves from predators. Well, they can't always, but all amphibians have poison glands in their skin, and many taste highly unpleasant. Predators learn to avoid them. Many are also well camouflaged and therefore hard to find.

An adult frog is carnivorous: it catches and feeds on live prey.

Amphibians have been around for at least 370 million years!

I know! But did you know that they evolved from fish?

PERFECT COLORS

Some amphibians have brightly patterned skin and that warns predators they are poisonous. Others change color to change their body temperature or to match their background for camouflage.

An amphibian's skin is not waterproof.

Tadpole to frog

All amphibians undergo a body change known as metamorphosis. Most begin life as an egg that develops into a larva. The Little Brainwaves are going to take a look at this process in a common frog.

ONE

Frogs (and toads) start life as eggs. These have a jellylike coating and clump together on a pond's surface as frog spawn. Each egg contains an embryo. A common frog will lay up to 2,000 eggs at one time.

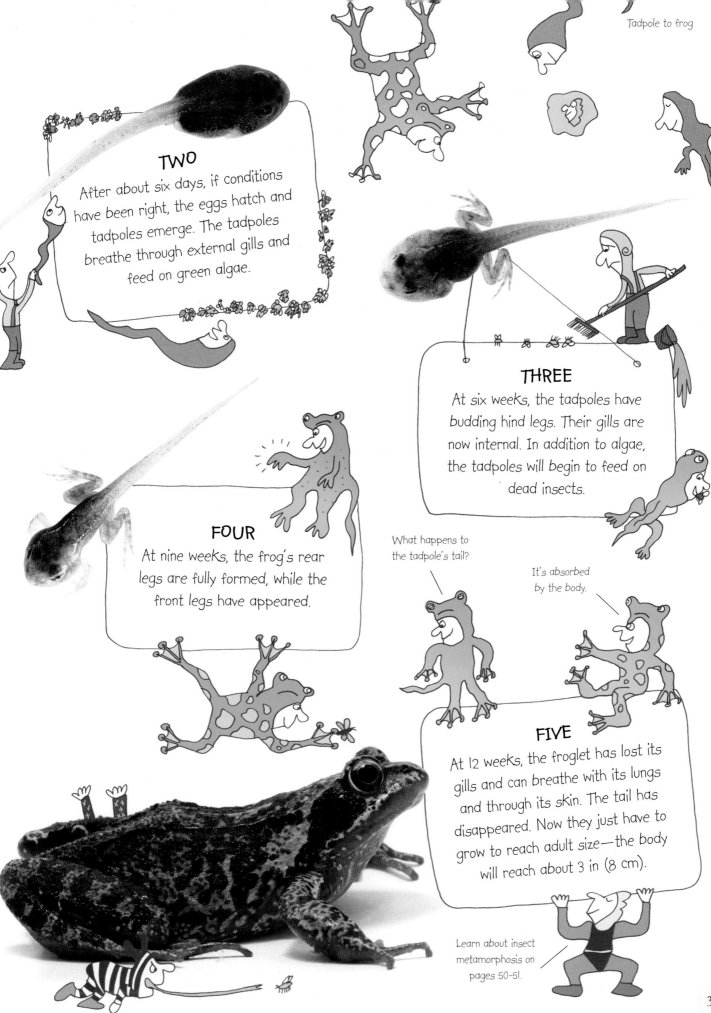

TWO

After about six days, if conditions have been right, the eggs hatch and tadpoles emerge. The tadpoles breathe through external gills and feed on green algae.

THREE

At six weeks, the tadpoles have budding hind legs. Their gills are now internal. In addition to algae, the tadpoles will begin to feed on dead insects.

FOUR

At nine weeks, the frog's rear legs are fully formed, while the front legs have appeared.

What happens to the tadpole's tail?

It's absorbed by the body.

FIVE

At 12 weeks, the froglet has lost its gills and can breathe with its lungs and through its skin. The tail has disappeared. Now they just have to grow to reach adult size—the body will reach about 3 in (8 cm).

Learn about insect metamorphosis on pages 50-51.

What is a fish?

More than half of all vertebrate (animals with backbones) species are fish. These animals are built for life in water, most having gills and a body covered with smooth, protective scales.

MADE FOR LIFE UNDER WATER

A fish's streamlined shape helps the animal to slip through the water, while gills allow it to breathe under the water.

Fish are cold-blooded.

The first vertebrates were primitive fish.

When did they appear?

More than 450 million years ago!

EARLY LIFE

All fish begin life as eggs. Some are laid in the water and hatch as larvae, others as tiny adults. Others, such as sharks, develop inside the body and are born as live young.

A bony flap protects the fish's gills.

Fish go to school!

No, they swim in schools! There's safety in numbers when they all swim together.

Brown trout eggs

FLEXIBLE FINS

Most fish swim using fins, but some use their fins for more than swimming. Some use their fins for walking along the seabed, while flying fish use theirs to glide briefly above the water's surface. Mudskippers use their front fins to crawl across mud.

Mudskipper

Fish scales form a protective layer.

HOW DOES A FISH BREATHE?

Fish use gills to remove oxygen from water to breathe (aside from lungfish, which can breathe directly from the air). What are gills? They are feathery structures found along the sides of the head, often protected by a bony flap.

Unusual fish

* Sea horses may not look like fish, but they are. They have tiny fins and tails that can grip onto plants or corals.

* Eels are long and snakelike in their appearance and behavior. Many eels have sharp teeth to grab prey.

* Rays have a flattened shape. Some are able to stun their prey—smaller fish—with a charge of electricity.

On the coral reef

The warm, shallow waters of a tropical coral reef are home to some of the most unusual and colorful fish in the world. Many of these swim together in schools of hundreds of fish.

SAFETY IN NUMBERS

These blue-striped snapper fish swim skillfully together, all heading in the same directions and turning at the same time. This makes it difficult for an enemy (a predator) to pick out a single fish to eat.

WHAT'S CORAL?

Coral is a type of tiny sea animal. Its home is a stony cup that it builds around itself. When the coral dies, the cup stays behind. Coral lives in huge colonies, with new animals making their cups on top of the ones that have died. Over time, they form coral reefs.

TIME TO GET BIGGER

Pufferfish have big ideas when it comes to escaping from an enemy. When threatened, they quickly fill their bodies with water, growing in size. When the danger has passed, they push the water out and go back to normal.

Why so colorful?

There's lots of color on a coral reef—animals and plants are bursting with it. They use it as camouflage, so they can hide from enemies, or to confuse enemies. Or they use it to signal to other fish.

* This copperband butterfly fish has a false eyespot to confuse predators.

* This trumpet fish changes color to match the fish it is swimming with.

* This little flasher wrasse flashes brilliant colors to attract a female.

LET'S GET CLEANED UP

Fish are covered in dead skin and scales as well as tiny animals called parasites. Sometimes they need to be cleaned! So they go to cleaning stations on the reef, where cleaner fish eat away the debris.

Killing machine

Sharks are feared by many, yet they rarely attack people. So why do they make people nervous? It's because of their teeth... in some species, all 3,000 of them. They are sharp and perfectly shaped for cutting and tearing.

OPEN WIDE!
Let's peep into the mouth of a great white shark, with its sharp, jagged-edged teeth arranged in three rows. When the shark loses a tooth, there is always another ready to move forward and take its place.

Instead, sharks tear off chunks of flesh and swallow it straight down.

Sharks can't chew their food. They don't have grinding teeth like us (our back teeth).

You're more likely to be struck by lightning than eaten by a shark.

Don't eat me!

SHARP TEETH
A closer look at a great white shark's tooth shows its jagged, or serrated, edge. This tooth is designed to cut and tear. Not all sharks have serrated teeth.

Egg-laying sharks lay their eggs in a protective pouch.

LITTLE SHARKS

Lots of sharks lay eggs, but most give birth to live young (called pups). A shark can have one to one hundred pups at a time, depending on what kind of shark it is. Sharks do not care for their eggs or pups. In fact, many sharks will eat their own pups if they swim too close.

WHAT'S FOR DINNER?

Sharks never sleep. They spend their time hunting. Some, such as the tiger shark, eat anything—from turtles, seals, and squid to tin cans, clothes, car tires, and license plates! Others are fussier— they take a bite, check the flavor, and swim away if it is not to their taste.

Different sharks

There are more than 300 kinds of shark. Let's take a look at a few of these.

* The shortfin mako is the fastest shark in the ocean. It can swim at 60 mph (100 kph).

* Angel sharks are flat (like a stingray) and bury themselves under sand to lie in wait for prey.

* Hammerhead sharks have eyes on the ends of their wide, flattened, hammer-shaped heads.

* Goblin sharks have long, pointed snouts and are rarely seen, since they patrol deep waters.

* Whale sharks are the world's largest shark. They can grow to be as long as a bus.

What is an invertebrate?

At least 95 percent of the known animal kingdom are invertebrates. These animals have no backbones or internal skeletons. From simple worms and sea sponges to insects that live in communities (such as bees), invertebrates are fun to watch and study.

Types of invertebrate

There are so many different types of invertebrate that scientists divide them into large groups. Here are a few of these groups (there are actually more than 30 of them).

* Annelida... include earthworms, leeches, and bristleworms. These invertebrates have bodies that are divided into segments.

* Arthopods... form the largest group of animal. They have a hard outer covering and jointed limbs. Insects and crustaceans are arthropods

* Cnidaria... include jellyfish and corals. All the animals in this group have tentacles with stinging cells that they use to catch their food.

* Echinodermata... live largely on the sea floor. Many have a prickly body. Sea stars, sea urchins, and sea cucumbers belong in this group.

* Porifera... the sponges. These are the simplest of all living animals. Adult sponges spend their lives in one place, fixed to a rock on the sea floor.

Many invertebrates live in the sea.

1 know, and many are microscopic.

Sponges look more like plants than the animals that they are!

HUMAN SPINE

Human beings have skeletons with backbones made up from bones called vertebrae. Invertebrates don't have bony skeletons, and they lack a backbone.

CLOSE RELATIONS

Snails are mollusks. These invertebrates have an amazing array of body shapes. Squids and octopuses are also mollusks.

What is an insect?

There are more than a million different kinds of insect. But what IS an insect? Join the Little Brainwaves to find out. (The main things to remember are that an insect has three parts to its body and six legs.)

HOW IT WORKS

An insect's body is made up of its head at one end, thorax in the middle, and abdomen at the other end. Its six legs are attached to the thorax. Its brain is in its head and its digestive system is in its abdomen.

There's an incredible variety of insects. What am I pretending to be?

You're an ant! Did you know that lots of insects have wings. Flies are insects.

Family groups

Insects can be split into groups of similar insects (too many to list here). They include:

The five largest groups:
*Beetles
*Bugs
*Flies
*Wasps, ants, and bees
*Butterflies and moths

as well as:
*Termites
*Earwigs
*Cockroaches
*Dragonflies
*Grasshoppers and crickets

Hoverfly (Eristalis)

Earwig (Dermaptera)

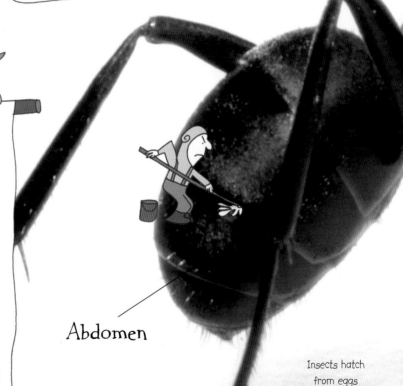

Abdomen

Insects hatch from eggs

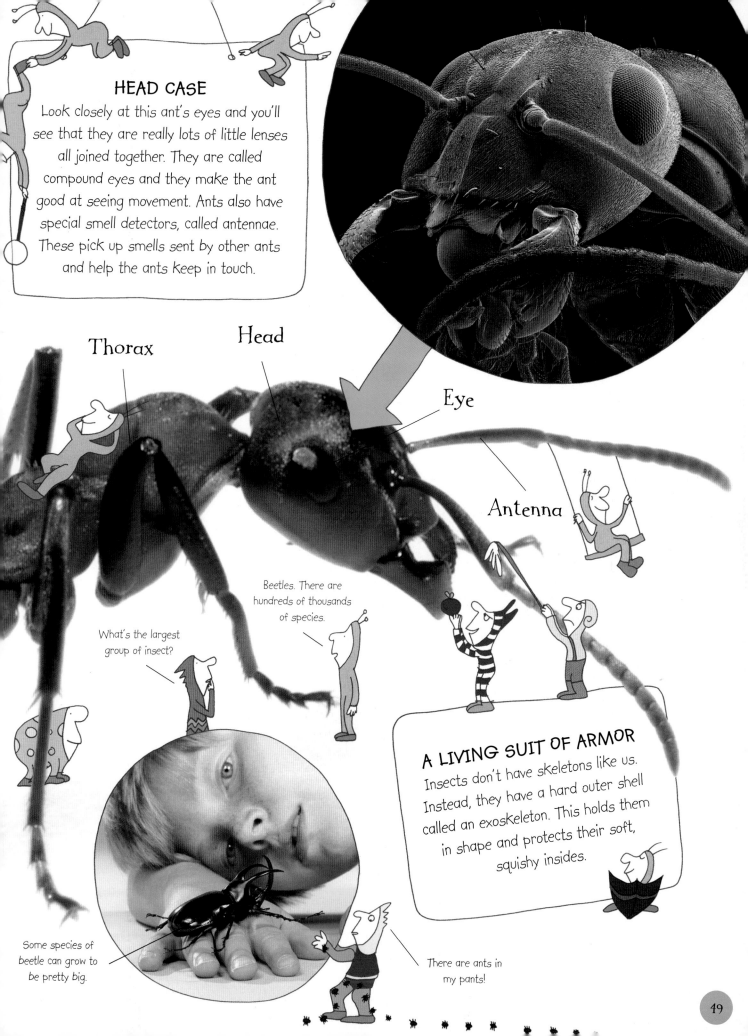

HEAD CASE

Look closely at this ant's eyes and you'll see that they are really lots of little lenses all joined together. They are called compound eyes and they make the ant good at seeing movement. Ants also have special smell detectors, called antennae. These pick up smells sent by other ants and help the ants keep in touch.

Thorax

Head

Eye

Antenna

What's the largest group of insect?

Beetles. There are hundreds of thousands of species.

A LIVING SUIT OF ARMOR

Insects don't have skeletons like us. Instead, they have a hard outer shell called an exoskeleton. This holds them in shape and protects their soft, squishy insides.

Some species of beetle can grow to be pretty big.

There are ants in my pants!

A butterfly emerges

Insects start life as eggs and then go through different stages before reaching their adult form. Many undergo a complete change in appearance. It's known as "metamorphosis." One insect that undergoes metamorphosis is the butterfly.

ONE

Butterfly eggs are laid on leaves or stems, usually on or near the intended caterpillar food.

An empty chrysalis is a sign a butterfly has emerged.

TWO

The caterpillar's job is to eat and grow, and to keep from being eaten. A caterpillar (or larva) often has a pattern of stripes or patches that helps it to hide. Some have spinelike hairs. As it grows, it sheds its skin four or more times so as to enclose its rapidly growing body.

THREE

A chrysalis (or pupa) is the stage in which the caterpillar changes. Inside this hard case, the caterpillar's tissues break down and the adult insect forms. Most butterflies have a brown or green chrysalis that helps them blend into the background.

Chrysalis

After it breaks out of its chrysalis, a butterfly has to let its wings dry before it can fly.

FOUR

The adult (the "imago") can both fly and reproduce. The adults spend their time looking for a mate and laying eggs. Some butterflies travel a long way after they emerge.

Look closer: bees

Busy bees. They buzz around the yard and can inflict a nasty sting. But don't worry, bees are actually the good guys—especially if you are a flower.

Bees carry pollen in baskets on their back legs.

A BEE'S WORK
The bee is a flower's best friend. Bees transfer pollen from flower to flower and that allows the flowers to reproduce.

They take the pollen back to the hive to feed their young.

SO MUCH TO DO
A bee will visit between 50 and 100 flowers on each flying trip. It takes the nectar from two million flowers to make 1 lb (450 g) of honey. No wonder honeybees are so busy.

A single honeybee will produce just one-twelfth of a teaspoon of honey in its lifetime!

Bees are furry, which is how you can tell them from wasps. Bumblebees are hairier than honeybees.

OUCH!

Bees only sting if they are attacked or upset. Worker honeybees have a barbed sting, which is left in your skin after stinging. This results in the honeybee dying. Bumblebees don't die after stinging, and some bees don't sting at all.

Bee facts

* Bee head. The bee's sensitive antennae sit between its compound eyes, which are made up of more than 4,000 lenses.

* Food source. Bees visit flowers for the sweet nectar, which they eat. While collecting the nectar, the flower's pollen sticks to the bee.

* Waggle dance. Want directions to a new flower? The dance performed by honeybees tells the others how far it is and which way to go.

* Home fields. Farmers and beekeepers work together, using bees to pollinate crops and make honey. Some beekeepers move their hives onto farms.

WHY DOES IT BUZZ?

Bees fly at an average speed of 14 mph (22.5 km/h). They beat their wings about 180 times a minute when they're flying. This is what makes the buzzing sound.

Look closer: grasshoppers

There are about 10,000 species of grasshopper. They belong to the same family as crickets, but there are lots of differences between the two. For a start, grasshoppers are active in the day, while crickets come out at night.

THEY SING!

Stand in a field of grass and you will probably soon hear a grasshopper's song. They sing by rubbing a row of little pegs on their long hind legs against the sides of their wings. Only the males sing—they do it to attract females. Different species sing different songs.

Do grasshoppers have "ears" in their knees?

No, those are crickets. Grasshoppers have "ears" on the sides of their bodies.

YUM, YUM

Like most crickets, this one eats just about anything—from grass to maggots and insects. Grasshoppers, on the other hand, will only eat plant matter.

When a grasshopper is picked up, it spits a brown liquid.

Scientists think this is protection against ant attacks.

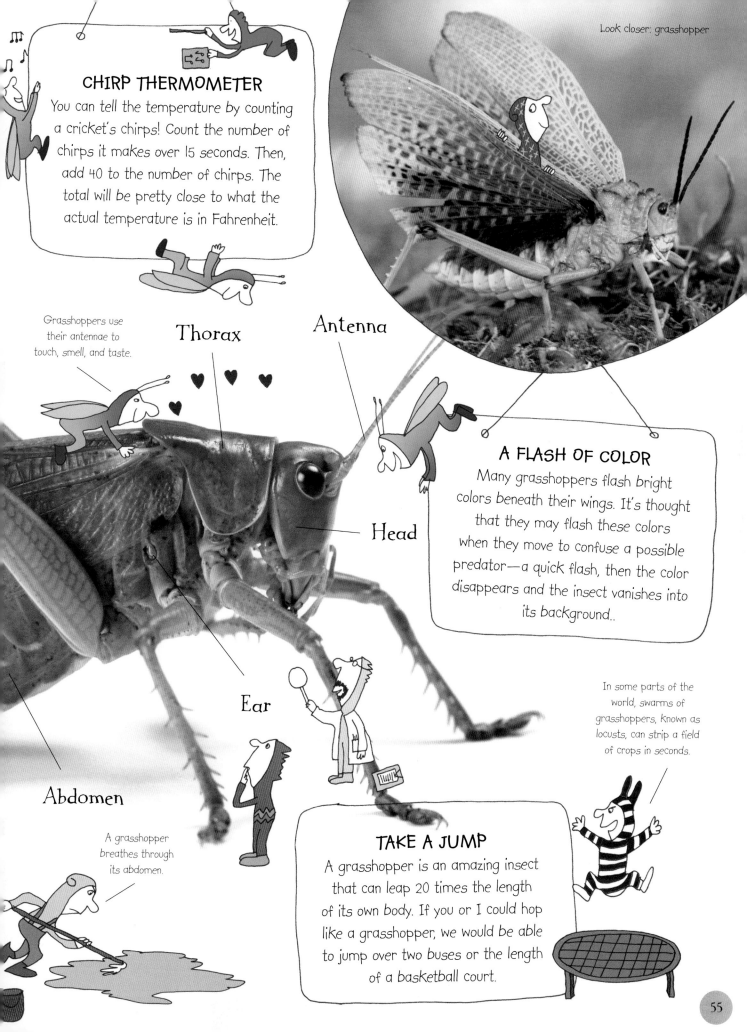

CHIRP THERMOMETER

You can tell the temperature by counting a cricket's chirps! Count the number of chirps it makes over 15 seconds. Then, add 40 to the number of chirps. The total will be pretty close to what the actual temperature is in Fahrenheit.

Grasshoppers use their antennae to touch, smell, and taste.

Thorax

Antenna

A FLASH OF COLOR

Many grasshoppers flash bright colors beneath their wings. It's thought that they may flash these colors when they move to confuse a possible predator—a quick flash, then the color disappears and the insect vanishes into its background..

Head

Ear

In some parts of the world, swarms of grasshoppers, known as locusts, can strip a field of crops in seconds.

Abdomen

A grasshopper breathes through its abdomen.

TAKE A JUMP

A grasshopper is an amazing insect that can leap 20 times the length of its own body. If you or I could hop like a grasshopper, we would be able to jump over two buses or the length of a basketball court.

What is an arachnid?

This massive group of arthropods includes spiders and scorpions, as well as tiny ticks and mites. How do you tell something is an arachnid? For a start, nearly all arachnids have eight legs and two main body parts.

The eight legs are attached to the front part of an arachnid's body.

GOING HUNTING!

Lots of arachnids hunt living prey, biting or stinging to kill or paralyze. They use limblike mouthparts, called pedipalps, to hold their food. Ticks, however, stab into their prey and suck up blood.

Pedipalp

DRIBBLE, DRIBBLE

Most arachnids have small mouths and cannot chew food. They get around this by dribbling digestive fluid onto their prey to dissolve it into a pulp. They can then suck up the juices.

All arachnids are flesh (or blood) eaters, although mites often feed on plants.

WE ARE THE BIGGEST!

Spiders form the largest group of arachnids. There are more than 40,000 known species of spider.

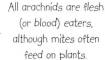

No arachnid has wings or antennae.

You're an insect!

What am I then?

A SCORPION

What is an arachnid?

The sting has a pair of venom glands at its base.

Pedipalp

Most arachnids live on land.

SCORPION ALERT!
Scorpions are the among the most ancient of all arachnids. Their pincer pedipalps are used to catch and hold their prey, while the end of the tail delivers a venomous sting to paralyze the scorpion's victim.

Eeeeek... I'm scared of spiders!

Say hello to Mr. Spider!

IT'S GOT TOO MANY LEGS!
Some people are scared of spiders and other arachnids. Being scared of spiders is called arachnophobia.

Did you know...?
... that ticks and mites are related to spiders? They are arachnids, too.

* Ticks are blood-suckers. They swell as they take in blood.

* Mites are all around us, but they are tiny and go unseen.

Amazing animals

Scientists believe there may be more than 10 million species, or types, of animal, but fewer than two million have been described. Take a look at some of the amazing facts that help to make the world of animals so incredible.

THE SIBERIAN TIGER

This tiger, *Panthera tibris altaica*, is the largest member of the cat family. An adult male can reach the weight of about 12 nine-year-old children.

FOOD TALK

Do you eat three times a day? Many animals eat far less frequently, especially reptiles. A crocodile needs a good meal just once a week and can go without food for longer, if necessary!

Potter wasp

Giant ichneumon wasp

HUNGRY LION

An adult male lion will eat the equivalent of some 650 sausages at one meal. An adult female will eat far less—the equivalent of about 375 sausages.

MOST POISONOUS VERTEBRATE

The GOLDEN poison FROG (*Phyllobates terribilis*) is the most poisonous of all vertebrates: the poison contained within just one frog could kill up to 20 people. Most animals know to avoid it—but one species of frog-eating snake is resistant to the poison.

DON'T STICK OUT YOUR TONGUE!

A giant anteater will flick out its tongue 150 times a minute when it's feeding at an ant's nest.

I SMELL LUNCH

A shark can detect a few drops of blood in an area of water the size of a Olympic-sized swimming pool.

A FULLY GROWN BLUE WHALE, THE WORLD'S LARGEST ANIMAL, IS AS LONG AS 19 DIVERS SWIMMING HEAD TO FOOT.

SMALLEST BIRD

The smallest bird in the world, the bee hummingbird, is tiny enough to perch happily on top of a pencil. It weighs just 1/16th oz (2 g).

A little bit of history!

c. 4th century BCE ARISTOTLE (384 to 322 BCE) divided living things into two groups: plants and animals. He divided animals into three groups according to how they moved—walking, flying, or swimming. This system was used until the 1600s.

In the 18th century, Swedish scientist Carolus Linnaeus (1707-1778) divided living things into two kingdoms: plants and animals, and divided each kingdom into small groups called genera. Genera were divided into species. His system gave each living thing a unique name.

1859 Charles Darwin (1809-82) published *On the Origin of Species*, which changed the way people saw the natural world.

Glossary

AMPHIBIAN: An animal that may live on land or in the water and that lays shell-less eggs.

ANTENNA (plural **ANTENNAE**): One of a pair of long sense organs found on an arthropod's head. They are used to feel, taste, and smell; they are also useful in picking up vibrations.

ARACHNID: A group of invertebrates that has eight legs.

ARTHROPOD: An invertebrate with a hard body casing (exoskeleton) and jointed legs.

CAMOUFLAGE: A color or pattern that helps an animal blend into its background so that it can't be seen.

CARNIVORE: An animal that eats meat.

CHRYSALIS: The protective case of a pupa.

COLD-BLOODED: An animal that cannot maintain its body temperature and that has to rely on the Sun's heat to warm up or find shade in which to cool down.

COMPOUND EYE: An eye made up of hundreds of tiny units, each of which makes a separate image.

EGG TOOTH: A horny growth on a chick's bill that is used to break through the shell to allow the chick to hatch. The egg tooth soon disappears.

EMBRYO: An animal in the very early stages of its growth, before it has hatched or been born.

EXOSKELETON: An arthropod's hard outer skeleton.

FOOD CHAIN: The transfer of energy from the Sun to a plant to the animal that eats it, and so on.

GILLS: Feathery structures on the side of a fish's head. Fish use gills to take oxygen from the water in order to breathe.

GNAW: To bite or nibble continuously.

HERBIVORE: An animal that eats only plants and their fruits and seeds.

INSECT: A group of invertebrate that has six legs and three body parts.

INVERTEBRATE: Animals without backbones. Mollusks are invertebrates.

KERATIN: A tough protein found in hair, nails, claws, hooves, and horns.

LARVA (plural **LARVAE**): The young stage of an insect, amphibian, or cnidarian. Larvae look very different from adults.

MAMMAL: An animal that feeds its young on milk.

METAMORPHOSIS: The change in body form that some animals, such as amphibians and butterflies, undergo before becoming adults.

NECTAR: A sugary liquid made by plants.

PEDIPALPS: An arachnid's limblike appendages, positioned by its mouth.

POLLEN: A dustlike powder produced by flowers.

PREDATOR: An animal that kills and eats other animals.

PREENING: The way a bird cleans and oils its feathers with its beak.

PREHENSILE TAIL: A tail that can grasp.

PREY: The animal that is killed and eaten by a predator.

PRIDE: A group of lions.

PRIMATE: A mammal, such as an ape or monkey, with forward-facing eyes and opposable thumbs.

RODENT: A group of mammals, including rats and mice, that have a pair of sharp front teeth for gnawing.

SPECIES: A group of living things that can breed together in the wild.

STALKING: The creeping behavior of a predator approaching its prey.

SUCKLE: The means by which a baby mammal takes milk from its mother by suckling a teat.

TALONS: The claws of a bird of prey such as an eagle.

VENOM: A harmful liquid produced by some animals (such as snakes) and delivered by a bite or a sting.

VERTEBRATE: Animals with backbones. Apes are vertebrates.

Index

Picture credits

The publisher would like to thank the following for their kind permission to reproduce their photographs: (Key: a-above; b-below/bottom; c-center; f-far; l-left; r-right; t-top)

Alamy Images: Arco Images GmbH / M. Delpho 26-27; Dave Bevan 46cl (worm); Blickwinkel / Schmidbauer 41bc; John Cancalosi 11br; Simon Colmer and Abby Rex 38-39; Michael Dietrich / Imagebroker 41tr; Indian Gypsy 18-19; Images & Stories 43br; Juniors Bildarchiv / F326 43ca; Krishnan V 16clb; Microscan / PhotoTake 27cr; Ron Niebrugge 23crb; Vova Pomortzeff 43cr; Andre Seale 43crb; Adam Seward 13; Top-Pics TBK 26bl (robin); Travel South Africa - Chris Ridley 31tr; Travelib Africa 42bl; www.lifeonwhite.eu l. **Corbis:** Smailes Alex / Corbis Sygma 45cr; Theo Allofs 10clb; B. Borrell Casals / Frank Lane Picture Agency 58fclb; Gary W. Carter 58cb; Clouds Hill Imaging Ltd. 40bc; Digital Zoo 56-57, 57tr; DLILLC 12; Jack Goldfarb / Design Pics 36fclb; Herbert Kehrer 46-47; Frans Lanting 32-33, 33clb; Frank Lukasseck 15tr; Michael Maloney / San Francisco Chronicle 53crb; Don Mason 53t; Amos Nachoum 23bl; Pat O'Hara 25tl; Image Plan 20-21; Jeffrey L. Rotman 11tr; Karlheinz Schindler / DPA 53br; Denis Scott 22-23; Sea Life Park / Handout / Reuters 45crb; Sea World of California 46clb; Stuart Westmorland 23cr; Tim Zurowski / All Canada Photos 48fbl. **Dorling Kindersley:** Natural History Museum, London 44clb. **Getty Images:** Botanica / Jami Tarris 25cr; Digital Vision / Baerbel Schmidt 49bl; Digital Vision / Justin Lewis 45br; David Fleetham / Visuals Unlimited, Inc. 23br, 42-43, 43tl; Flickr / Dene' Miles 26cl; Flickr / Vistas from Soni Rakesh 50-51; Gallo Images / Heinrich van den Berg 55tr; Gallo Images / Michael Langford 36clb; Iconica / Jeff Rotman 45crb (hammerhead); The Image Bank / Daisy Gilardini 21cra; The Image Bank / Steve Allen 26clb; The Image Bank / Tai Power Seeff 31fbr; The Image Bank / Theo Allofs 26cla; iStock Exclusive / Ina Peters 33tr; Lifesize / Angelo Cavalli 6-7; Lifesize / Charles Nesbit 47tr; Lifesize / Don Farrall 36-37; National Geographic / Brian J. Skerry 45bl; National Geographic / George Grall 41clb; National Geographic / Joel Sartore 59ca; National Geographic / Klaus Nigge 31br, 31fcrb; Oxford Scientific / Photolibrary 9tl; Photodisc / Alan and Sandy Carey 24cl; Photodisc / Gail Shumway 37crb; Photodisc / Paul Souders 21tc; Photodisc / Tom Brakefield 16-17; Photographer's Choice / Carlos Davila 46clb (starfish); Photographer's Choice / Joe Drivas 32br; Photographer's Choice / Paul Oomen 23br (walrus); Photographer's Choice / Siegfried Layda 26bl; Photolibrary / David B. Fleetham 8bl; Photolibrary / Mark Jones 32fbr; Photolibrary / Richard Herrmann 45cr (mako); Photonica / Theo Allofs 14crb; Riser / Joseph Van Os 21bl; Robert Harding World Imagery / Paul Allen 17tr; Stone / James Balog 14l; Stone / Michael Melford 19crb; Stone / Stephen Frink 22bl; Taxi / Peter Lilja 13tl; Visuals Unlimited / Brandon Cole 46cl; Visuals Unlimited / Dr. Dennis Kunkel 53cr; Visuals Unlimited / Rob & Ann Simpson 36fbl. **iStockphoto.com:** Karel Broz 48-49; Victoria Omelianchyk 8-9; Kevin Panizza 46bl; Lee Pettet 38; Terry Wilson 58-59; Tomasz Zachariasz 54-55. **Science Photo Library:** Georgette Douwma 41c; Eye Of Science 57crb; Steve Gschmeissner 49tr, 57br; Anthony Mercieca 30-31; Gary Meszaros 48bl; Laurie O'Keefe 29r; Power and Syred 27tl.

Jacket images: Front: Alamy Images: www.lifeonwhite. eu. Back: Alamy Images: Indian Gypsy cla. Getty Images: David Fleetham / Visuals Unlimited, Inc. cr.

All other images © Dorling Kindersley
For further information see:
www.dkimages.com